For Katy, Alex and Zoë — C.B.

First published 2007 by Walker Books Ltd 87 Vauxhall Walk, London SE11 5HJ

1 2 3 4 5 6 7 8 9 10   Text © 1981 Naomi Lewis First published in HANS ANDERSEN'S FAIRY TALES in the United Kingdom by Puffin Books, 1981 Illustrations © 2007 Christian Birmingham The right of Naomi Lewis and Christian Birmingham to be identified as author and illustrator of this work has been asserted by them in accordance with the Copyright, Designs and Patents Act 1988 This book has been typeset in Futura T Light Printed in China All rights reserved. No part of this book may be reproduced, transmitted or stored in an information retrieval system in any form or by any means, graphic, electronic or mechanical, including photocopying, taping and recording, without prior written permission from the publisher. British Library Cataloguing in Publication Data: a catalogue record for this book is available from the British Library ISBN 978-1-4063-0634-7

www.walkerbooks.co.uk

The Snow Queen

Hans Christian Andersen

Naomi Lewis ✻ *Christian Birmingham*

PART ONE
Which Tells of the Looking-Glass and the Splinters

———❖———

Listen now! We're going to begin our story.

WHEN WE COME TO THE END OF IT we shall know more than we do now. There was once a wicked imp, a demon, one of the very worst – he was the Devil himself. One day, there he was, laughing his head off. Why? Because he had made a magic mirror with a special power; everything good and beautiful that was reflected in it shrivelled up almost to nothing, but everything evil and ugly seemed even larger, and more hideous than it was. In this glass, the loveliest landscapes looked just like boiled spinach, and even the nicest people appeared quite horrible, or seemed to be standing on their heads, or to have no trunks to their bodies. As for their faces, they were so twisted and changed that no one could have recognized them; and, if anything holy and serious passed through someone's mind, a hideous sneering grin was shown in the glass. This was a huge joke.

All the students who attended his Demon School went around declaring that he'd achieved a miracle; now everyone could see what the world and its humans were really like. They took the mirror and ran around to the four corners of the earth, until there wasn't a place or person unharmed by the glass.

At last they fixed on a still more daring plan – to fly up to heaven, to make fun of the angels, and of God himself. The higher they flew with the mirror, the more it grimaced and twisted; they could scarcely hold on to it. Up and up they went, nearer and nearer to heaven's kingdom – until, disaster! The mirror shook so violently with its weird reflections that it sprang out of their hands and went crashing down to earth, where it burst into hundreds of millions, billions, trillions of tiny pieces. And that made matters even worse than before, for some of these pieces were hardly as big as a grain of sand. These flew here and there, all through the wide world; whoever got a speck in his eye saw everything good as bad or twisted – for every little splinter had the same power that the whole glass had. Some people even caught a splinter in their hearts, and that was horrible, for their hearts became just like lumps of ice. Some of the pieces were so big that they were used as window panes – but it didn't do to look at your friends through them. Other pieces were made into spectacles – imagine! The demon laughed till he nearly split his sides.

And, as we tell this story, little splinters of magic glass are still flying about in the air. Listen! You shall hear what happened to some of them ✶

PART TWO
A Little Boy and a Little Girl

◆━━━◆━━━◆

IN A BIG CITY, where there are so many houses and people that there isn't room for everyone to have a garden, and so most people have to make do with flowers in pots, there once lived two poor children. But these two did have a garden a little larger than a flowerpot.

They were not brother and sister, but they were just as fond of each other as if they had been. Their parents were next-door neighbours; they lived in attics at the tops of next-door houses. Where the sloping roofs almost touched, a gutter ran along between; and across this, each house had a little window facing the other. You had only to step along the strip of roof to cross from window to window.

The parents each had a wooden box standing outside the window, and here they grew vegetables and herbs. They had little rose trees too, one in each box, and these grew gloriously. The pea plants trailed over the edges; the rose trees put out long branches, some twining around the windows, some bending over towards the opposite bush, making a kind of arch of leaves and flowers. The children would often sit on their little wooden stools under the roof of roses, and talk and play and spend many a happy hour.

In the winter, of course, there was no sitting out on the roof. The windows were often thick with frost, but the two children would warm up a coin on the stove, then press it on the frozen pane. This would make a splendid peep-hole. Behind each round hole was a bright and friendly eye, one at each window. These were the eyes of the little boy and the little girl; his name was Kay and hers was Gerda. In summer they could be together with a single jump, but in winter they first had to climb all the way down one set of stairs, then up another – while outside the snow fell fast.

"Those are the white bees swarming," said the old grandmother.

"Have they a queen too?" asked the little boy, for he knew that real bees have.

"Yes, indeed," said the grandmother. "Wherever the flakes swarm most thickly, there she flies; she is the largest of them all.

She never lies still on the ground, though, but soars up once again into the black cloud. On many a winter night she flies through the streets of the town and peers in at the windows, and then they freeze into the strangest patterns, like stars and flowers."

"Yes, I've seen that!" both children cried at once, knowing now that it must be true.

"Could the Snow Queen come in here?" asked the little girl.

"Just let her try!" said the boy. "I'll put her on the hot stove and then she'll melt."

But the grandmother smoothed his hair, and told them other stories.

In the evening, when little Kay was back at home and half undressed, he climbed onto the chair by the window and looked out through the little hole. A few snowflakes were drifting outside; then one of these, much larger than the rest, settled on the edge of the window-box outside. This snowflake grew and grew until it seemed to take the shape of a lady dressed in the finest white gauze, which was in fact made up of millions of tiny starlike flakes. She was so beautiful, wonderfully delicate and grand; but she was ice all through, dazzling, glittering ice – and yet she was alive. Her eyes blazed out like two bright stars, but there was no peace or rest in them. Now she nodded towards the window, and beckoned with her hand. The little boy was frightened and jumped down from the chair, and then he thought he saw a great bird go flying past.

The next day was clear and frosty; after that the thaw began; then it was spring. The sun shone; the first green shoots appeared; swallows built their nests; the windows were thrown open and the two children sat once more in their little roof garden.

The roses were so beautiful that summer, more than ever before. The little girl had learnt a hymn which had a line about roses, and this made her think of her own. She sang the verse to the little boy, and he sang it too:

> *"In the vale the rose grows wild;*
> *Children play all the day –*
> *One of them is the Christ-child."*

How lovely the summer was. The rose garden seemed as if it would never stop flowering.

Kay and Gerda were looking at a picture book of birds and animals, and then – just as the clock in the great church tower began to strike five – Kay said, "Oh! Something pricked me in my heart! Oh! Now I've got something in my eye!"

The little girl put her arm round his neck, and he blinked his eyes. But no, there was nothing to be seen.

"I think it's gone," he said. But it hadn't. It was one of those tiny splinters from the demon's looking-glass – I'm sure you remember it. Poor Kay! He had got another piece right in his heart, which would soon be like a lump of ice. He didn't feel it, but it was there all right.

"Why are you crying?" he asked. "It makes you look horribly ugly. There's nothing the matter with me. Ugh!" he cried suddenly. "That rose has a worm in it. And look at that one – it's crooked. They're rotten, all of them. And the boxes, too." Then he kicked the boxes hard and tore off the two roses.

"Kay, what are you doing?" cried the little girl. And when he saw how frightened she was, he tore off a third rose, and ran in at his window, away from his little friend Gerda.

After that, when she brought out the picture book, he said that it was baby stuff. When the grandmother told them stories, he would always find fault, and argue. He would even walk close behind her, put on spectacles, and mimic her way of talking. It was so well done that it made the people laugh. Soon he could mimic the ways of everyone in the street, especially if they were odd or unpleasant. People used to say, "Oh, he's clever, that boy!" but all this came from the splinters of glass in his eye and in his heart; they made him tease even little Gerda, who loved him more than anything in the world.

His games had become quite different now; they were so scientific and practical. One winter's day, as the snowflakes drifted down, he brought out a magnifying glass, then held out the corner of his blue jacket to catch some falling flakes.

"Now look through the glass, Gerda," he said. And she saw that every flake was very much larger, and looked like a splendid flower or a ten-pointed star. It was certainly a wonderful sight. "Look at that pattern – isn't it marvellous!" said Kay. "These are much more interesting than real flowers – and there isn't a single fault in them. They're perfect – if only they didn't melt."

A little later Kay came back wearing big gloves and carrying his sledge on his back. He shouted into Gerda's ear, "They're letting me go tobogganing in the town square where the others are playing!" And away he went.

Out in the square the boldest boys would often tie their sleds to farmers' carts, and so be pulled along for quite a ride. It was enormous fun. This time, while their games were in full swing, a very large sledge arrived; it was painted white all over, and in it sat a figure muffled up in a white fur cloak and wearing a white fur hat. This sledge drove twice round the square; but, moving quickly, Kay managed to fix his own sledge behind it, and a swift ride began. The big sledge went faster and faster, then turned off into the next street. The driver looked round and nodded to Kay in the friendliest fashion, just as if they had always known each other. Every time that Kay thought of unfastening his sledge, the driver would turn and nod to him again, so he kept still. On they drove, straight out of the city gates. And now the snow began to fall so thick and fast that the little boy couldn't even see his hand in front of him as they rushed along. At last he did manage to untie the rope but it was of no use; his little sledge still clung to the big one, and they sped along like the wind. He cried out at the top of his voice, but no one heard him; the snow fell, and the sledge raced on. From time to time it seemed to jump, as if they were going over dykes and hedges. Terror seized him; he tried to say the Lord's Prayer, but all he could remember was the multiplication table.

The snowflakes grew bigger and bigger, until at last they looked like great white birds. All at once they swerved to one side; the sledge came to a halt, and the driver stood up. The white fur cloak and cap were all of snow and the driver – ah, she was a lady, tall and slender, dazzlingly white! She was the Snow Queen herself.

"We've come far and fast," she said. "But you must be frozen. Creep under my bearskin cloak." She put him beside her in the sledge and wrapped the cloak around him; he felt as if he were sinking into a snowdrift. "Are you still cold?" she asked, and she kissed him on the forehead. Ah-h-h! Her kiss was colder than ice; it went straight to his heart, which was already halfway to being a lump of ice. He felt as if he were dying, but only for a moment. Then he felt perfectly well, and no longer noticed the cold.

"My sledge! Don't forget my sledge!" That was the first thought that came to him. So it was tied to one of the big white birds, which flew along with the little sledge at its back. The Snow Queen kissed Kay once again, and after that he had no memory of Gerda and the grandmother, nor of anyone at home.

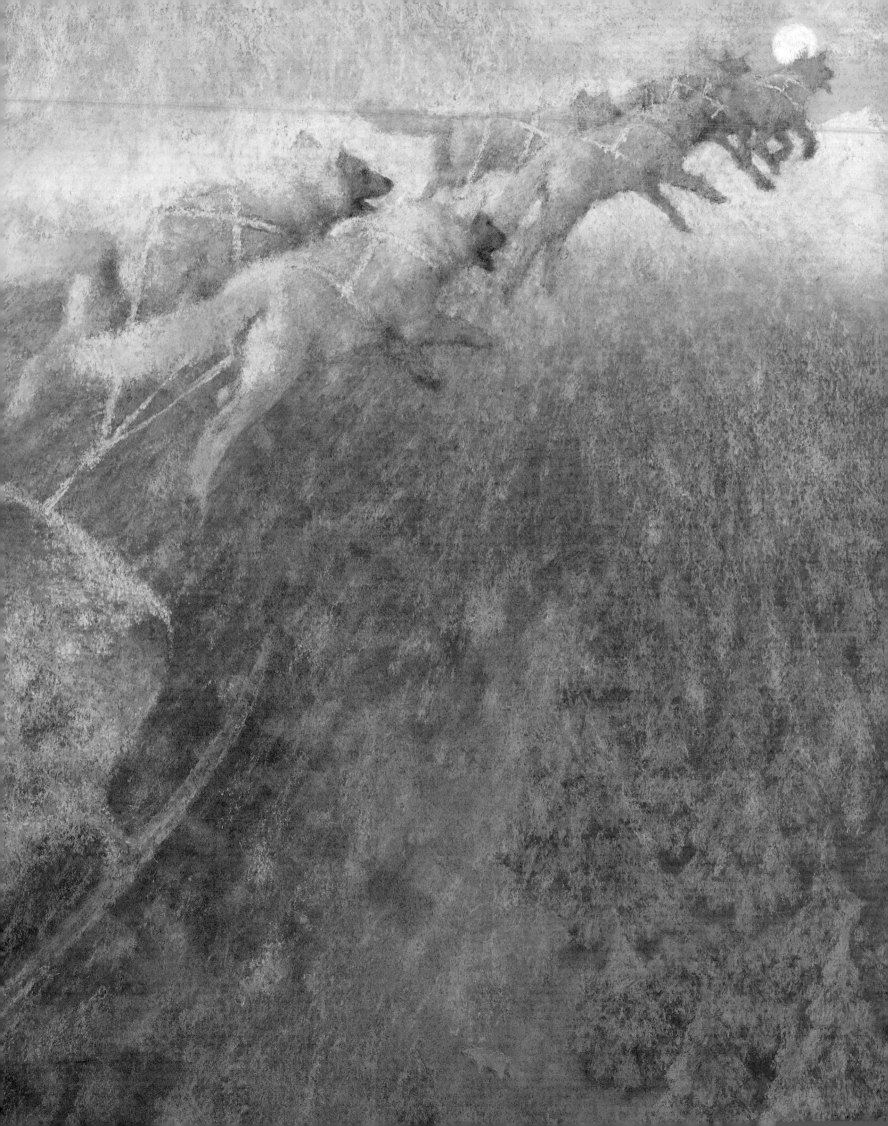

"Now I must give you no more kisses," said the Snow Queen, "or you will be kissed to death."

Kay looked at her. She was so beautiful; he could not imagine a wiser, lovelier face. She no longer seemed to him to be made of ice, as she once had seemed when she came to the attic window and waved to him. Now in his eyes she was perfect, and he felt no fear. He told her that he could do mental arithmetic, and fractions too; that he knew the square miles of all the principal countries, and the number of inhabitants. As he talked she smiled at him, until he began to think that what he knew was, after all, not quite so much. And he looked up into the vast expanse of the sky, as they rose up high, and she flew with him over the dark clouds, while the storm-wind whistled and raved, making him think of ballads of olden time. Over forest and lake they flew, over sea and land; beneath them screamed the icy blast; the wolves howled, the snow glittered; the black crows soared across the plains, cawing as they went. But high over all shone the great clear silver moon, and Kay gazed up at it all through the long, long winter night. During the day he slept at the Snow Queen's feet ✳

PART THREE
The Enchanted Flower Garden of the Old Woman who Understood Magic

BUT WHAT OF LITTLE GERDA when Kay did not return? Where could he be? No one knew; no one had any idea. The only thing that the boys could say was that they had seen him tie his little sledge to a big one, which drove out into the street and through the city gate. But who could tell what happened after that? There was great grief in the town; little Gerda wept many tears. Then people began to say that he must be dead, that he had fallen into the river that flowed past the city walls. Oh, what a long dark winter it was!

At last came the spring, and the first warm sunshine.

"Kay is dead and gone," said little Gerda.

"I don't believe it," said the sunshine.

"He is dead and gone," she said to the swallows.

"I don't believe it," declared each of the swallows. And at last little Gerda didn't believe it either. "I will put on my new red shoes," she said one morning, "the ones Kay has never seen, and I'll go down and ask the river."

It was still very early when she kissed her sleeping grandmother, put on the red shoes, and walked all alone through the city gate and down to the river.

"Is it true that you have taken my little playmate?" she said. "I'll give you my red shoes if you'll let me have him back."

The waves, she thought, nodded back to her very strangely. So she took off her red shoes, the most precious thing she owned, and threw them into the water. But they fell close to the bank, and the little waves carried them straight back to her. It seemed just as if the river would not accept her dearest possession because it hadn't taken little Kay. But then Gerda felt that perhaps she hadn't thrown the shoes out far enough, so she climbed into a boat that lay among the rushes, and went to the further end of it, and threw the shoes again. But the boat had not been moored fast, and the movement made it float away from the shore. It began to glide away, gathering speed all the time.

At this little Gerda was very much frightened and began to cry, only nobody heard her except the sparrows, and they couldn't carry her ashore. But they flew along the bank, singing as if to comfort her, "Here we are! Here we are!" On sped the boat while little Gerda sat quite still in her stockinged feet. Her red shoes floated behind, but they couldn't catch the boat, which was now moving faster and faster.

The scene was pretty enough on both sides of the water; there were lovely flowers, old trees, and grassy meadows with sheep and cows, but there wasn't a person in sight.

Perhaps the river is carrying me to little Kay, thought Gerda, and her spirits began to rise. She stood up, and gazed for hour after hour at the beautiful green banks. At last she came to a cherry orchard, in which stood a little house with curious red and blue windows and a thatched roof; standing outside were two wooden soldiers, presenting arms whenever anyone passed. Gerda called out to them, thinking that they were alive, but of course they gave no

answer. The river seemed to be driving the boat towards the bank, and Gerda called out even more pleadingly.

Then, from the cottage, came an old, old woman, leaning on a crutch-shaped stick. She wore a large sunhat, painted all over with many kinds of lovely flowers.

"You poor little child!" said the old woman. "How ever did you come to be on this river, so far out in the wide world?" And she stepped into the water, hooked the boat with her crooked stick, pulled it ashore, and lifted little Gerda down.

"Now come and tell me who you are," said she, "and how you managed to reach my house."

So Gerda told her everything, and the old woman shook her head and murmured, "Hm, hm!" And when Gerda had finished her tale, and asked if she had seen little Kay, the woman said that he hadn't yet passed by, but he was sure to come; she was not to worry, but to have a taste of her cherries, and see her flowers, which were more wonderful than any picture book; every one of them had a story to tell. Then she took Gerda into the little house and locked the door.

The windows were very high up, and the glass in them was red and yellow and blue. The daylight shone very strangely into the room with all these colours. But on the table were the most delicious cherries, and Gerda was told that she might eat as many as she liked. While she was eating, the old woman combed her hair with a golden comb, and her hair curled fair and shining round her little face that was just like a rose.

"I've often thought I would fancy a nice little girl around, just like you," said the old woman. "We shall get on very well together, you shall see." And she combed away at Gerda's hair, and as she combed, the little girl was forgetting more and more her playmate Kay. For the old woman could manage a bit of magic, though she was by no means a wicked witch. She used her magic only now and then for her own pleasure – and just now her pleasure was to keep little Gerda. To make sure of this, she went out into the garden and pointed her stick at each of the lovely rose-bushes; at once, each bush sank down into the black earth, as if it had never been. For the old woman feared that if Gerda saw the roses she would think of her own in the roof-boxes, and remember little Kay, and run off to take up her journey.

This done, she took Gerda out into the flower garden. Ah, that garden – you can't imagine what magical beauty and fragrance she found there. All the flowers that you could ever bring to mind were growing together in full bloom at one time. It was better than all the picture books. Gerda jumped with joy and played there until the sun went down behind the tall cherry trees. Then she was given a lovely bed, its red silk pillows stuffed with violets, and here she slept.

When morning came she went out again to play among the flowers in the radiant sunshine, and so many days were spent.

Before long she knew every separate flower, and yet, although there were so many, she felt that one was missing – only she could not think which. Then one day, as she was sitting indoors, her eyes turned to the painted flowers on the old woman's sunhat; the loveliest of all was a rose. The old woman had quite forgotten this when she had made the real ones disappear into the ground. See what happens when you don't keep your wits about you!

"Oh!" cried Gerda. "Why have I never seen any roses in the garden?" And she ran in and out of the flower beds, searching and searching, but not a rose was to be found.

At last she sat down and cried; but her warm tears fell just where a rose tree had sunk down. At once the tree sprang up, as full of fresh flowers as when it disappeared. Gerda put her arms around it, and kissed the roses, and thought about those in the roofgarden of her home – and then she remembered Kay.

"Oh, what a lot of time I have lost!" said the little girl. "I set out to find Kay. Do you know where he is?" she asked the roses. "Do you think he is dead and gone?"

"No, he is not dead," said the roses. "We have been in the earth where the dead are, but Kay was not there."

"Oh, thank you," said Gerda; then she went over to the other flowers, and looked into their cups, and asked, "Do you know where little Kay is?"

But the flowers stood in the sun, each one dreaming its own story. And Gerda listened to all the tales and dreams, but of Kay there was never a word.

What did the convolvulus say?

"High above, overlooking the narrow mountain road, stands an ancient castle. Evergreen creepers grow thickly over the old red walls; leaf by leaf they twine round the balcony where a fair young girl leans over the balustrade, gazing down at the path below. No rose on its branch is fresher and lovelier; no apple blossom that floats from the tree is more delicate. Listen – her silk dress rustles as she moves. 'When will he come?' she says."

"Is it Kay you mean?" asked little Gerda.

"I tell only my own story, my own dream," the convolvulus answered.

What did the little snowdrop say?

"Between the trees a board hangs by two ropes; it's a swing. Two pretty little girls in snow-white dresses sit swinging; long, green silk ribbons are fluttering from their hats. Their brother, who is bigger than they are, is standing up in the swing with his arm round the rope to keep himself steady, for in one hand he holds a little bowl and in the other a clay pipe; he is blowing soap bubbles. To and fro goes the swing, while the bubbles float away in a rainbow of changing colours; the last one still clings to the pipe and sways in the wind.

The swing still moves, to and fro.

The little black dog, as light as the bubbles, leaps up on his hind-legs; he wants to join the others on the swing. But it swoops past, out of reach, and the dog flops down, barking furiously. The children laugh; the bubbles burst. A swinging plank, a white flash of dissolving foam – that is my picture; that's my song."

"Your story may be beautiful, but you make it sound so sad, and you don't mention little Kay at all. Hyacinths, what have you to tell?"

"There were three lovely sisters, fragile, exquisite; one wore a dress of rose-red, the second of violet-blue, the third, pure white. Hand in hand they danced by the silent lake in the clear moonlight. They were not fairies, they were children of men. A sweet scent filled the air and the girls vanished into the wood. The fragrance grew more powerful; three coffins, in which lay three lovely girls, glided from the depths of the wood, over the lake; fireflies flew around them like tiny flickering lamps. Are the dancing maidens sleeping or are they dead? Perhaps, from the scent of the flowers, they are dead, and the bells are ringing for them."

"You make me feel dreadfully sad," said little Gerda. "And your own scent is so powerful that I can't help thinking of those sleeping girls. Can little Kay really be dead? The roses have been in the ground, and they say no."

"Ding dong!" rang out the hyacinth bells. "We're not ringing for little Kay; we don't know him. All we sing is our own song, the only one we know."

So Gerda went to the buttercup, which shone out from its fresh green leaves. "You are a bright little sun!" said Gerda. "Tell me if you know where I can find my playmate."

The buttercup shone very prettily, and looked up at Gerda. Now what song would the buttercup sing? Not one that gave her news of little Kay.

"In a small backyard the heavenly sun shone bright and warm; it was the first day of spring, and the sunbeams slid down the neighbour's whitewashed wall. Nearby, the first yellow flowers of spring were growing, gleaming just like gold in the golden rays. The old grandmother sat outside in her chair; her granddaughter, a poor servant girl, but pretty enough, had come home for a short visit, and now she kissed her grandmother. There was heart's gold in that kiss in the golden morning. That's all; there's my story."

"My poor old granny!" sighed Gerda. "I'm sure she's longing for me and grieving, just as she grieved about little Kay. But I'll soon be home again, and bring Kay with me. It's no use asking the flowers – their own tales are all they know, and they tell me nothing at all."

She tucked up her dress so that she could run fast, and away she went. Then something struck her leg quite smartly as she leapt over it; she looked – and it was a narcissus. Maybe you have news for me, she thought, and she bent down towards the flower.

"I see myself! I see myself!" said the narcissus. "Ah, what a sweet perfume! High up in her attic lodging is a little ballet dancer. She stands on tiptoe, now on one leg, now on the other, and kicks out at the world. It is all in the mind, you know. Now she pours water from the kettle onto a piece of cloth – it's her dancer's bodice; cleanliness is next to godliness, as they say. Her white dress hangs on a peg; that too has been washed, then hung on the roof to dry. Now she puts it on, and around her neck she ties a saffron-yellow scarf. It makes the dress seem even whiter. She raises one leg high in the air. How elegantly she stands and sways on her stalk! I see myself! I see myself!"

"That is your story, not mine," said Gerda. "I don't want to hear any more." She ran to the edge of the garden. The gate was locked, but she twisted the rusty fastening until it came away; the gate flew open and little Gerda ran out barefooted into the wide world. Three times she looked back, but nobody was following her. At last she could run no further, so she sat down on a big stone. As she gazed around her, she realized that summer was over; it was late autumn. There had been no signs of changing time in that enchanted garden, where the bright sun always shone and flowers of every season bloomed together.

"Oh, I have lingered here too long," said little Gerda. "Autumn has come; I dare not stop!" She got up from the stone and started off once more. How tired and sore her feet were! How cold and damp was the countryside! The long willow leaves had turned quite yellow and wet with mist; they dropped off one by one. Only the thorny sloe had kept its fruit, but that was so sour that the thought of it twisted your mouth. Oh, how mournful and bleak it was in the wide world! ❄

PART FOUR
Prince and Princess

—⟨⟨⟨⟨≫—

GERDA SOON HAD TO REST AGAIN. And there, hopping about in the snow, right in front of her, was a raven. He had been staring at her for some time, with his head on one side, then on the other. Now he greeted her "Caw, caw! How do, how do!" It may not have been an elegant way of speaking, but it was kindly meant. He asked her where she was going, all alone in the wide world. So she told the raven her story and asked if he had seen little Kay.

The raven nodded thoughtfully, and said, "Could be! Could be!"

"Oh – you really think that you have some news?" cried the little girl. And she hugged the bird so tightly that she nearly squeezed him to death.

"Caw, caw! Care-ful, care-ful!" the raven said. "I think that it may have been little Kay. But I fancy that by this time he will have forgotten you for the princess."

"Does he live with a princess?" asked Gerda.

"Now listen and I'll tell you," said the raven. "But I find it so hard to talk your language. If only you understood raven speech I could tell you better."

"No, I never learned that," said Gerda, "though my granny knew it and other strange things too. I only wish I did."

"Well, never mind," said the raven. "I'll tell you as plainly as I can; you can't ask for more." And then he related what he knew. "In the kingdom where we are now, a princess dwells. She is extremely clever; she has read all the newspapers in the world and has forgotten them again – that's how clever she is. She was sitting on her throne the other day when she happened to hear a little song. It goes like this: *Why should I not married be? Why not? Why not? Why not?* Well, there's something to

be said for that, she thought. So she decided to find a partner, but she wanted one who could speak for himself when spoken to – one who didn't just stand and look important. That's very dull. She ordered her ladies-in-waiting to be called together (it was done by sounding a roll of drums), and when they heard her plan they were delighted. 'What a splendid idea!' 'We were thinking something of the kind just the other day!' They went on making remarks like these. All that I'm telling you is perfectly true," said the raven. "I've a tame sweetheart who has a free run of the palace, and I heard the tale from her."

Need I tell you that the sweetheart was also a raven? Birds will be birds, and a raven's mate is a raven.

"The newspapers promptly came out with a border of hearts and the princess's monogram. They announced that any good-looking young man might come to the palace and meet the princess; the one who seemed most at home in the princess's company but who was also the best and most interesting talker – that was the one she meant to choose.

"Well, the suitors flocked to the palace – there never was such a crowd! But nobody won the prize, either the first day or the next. They could all talk smartly enough when they were out in the street, but when they came through the palace gate and saw the guards in their silver uniforms, and the footmen in gold all the way up the stairs, and the great halls with their brilliant lights, they seemed to be struck dumb. And when they stood before the throne where the princess sat, they could find nothing to say but the last word she had spoken herself, and she had no wish to hear that again. Though once they were back in the street, it was all chatter, chatter as before. There was a queue stretching away right from the city gate to the palace. I went over myself to have a look," said the raven.

"But Kay, little Kay!" asked Gerda. "When did he come? Was he in that crowd?"

"Give me time! Give me time! We're coming to him! It was on the third day when a little chap appeared without horse or carriage and stepped jauntily up to the palace. His eyes were shining, just like yours; he had fine thick flowing hair – but his clothes, I must say, were shabby."

"That was Kay!" cried Gerda. "Oh, I have found him at last!" And she clapped her hands with joy.

"He had a little knapsack or bundle on his back," said the raven.

"Ah, that must have been his sledge," said Gerda. "He had it when he left."

"It may have been," said the raven. "I didn't study it all that closely. But I do know from my tame sweetheart that when he reached the palace gate and saw the guards in silver and the footmen in gold, he was not in the least dismayed. He only nodded pleasantly and said to them, 'It must be dull work standing there; I'd sooner go inside.'

"The great halls blazed with light; it was enough to make anyone feel small. The young chap's boots squeaked dreadfully, but even this didn't trouble him."

"That's certainly Kay!" cried Gerda. "His boots were new, I know; I heard them squeaking in my grandmother's kitchen."

"Well, they squeaked, to be sure," said the raven. "But he went merrily up to the princess, who was sitting on a pearl as big as a spinning wheel; all the ladies-in-waiting, with their maids and their maids'

maids, and all the gentlemen courtiers, with their serving

men and their serving men's serving men, were arranged around her in order.

"But did Kay win the princess?" asked little Gerda.

"If I hadn't been a bird I would have had a try myself, betrothed or not

betrothed," the raven said. "He is said to have spoken as well as I do when I speak

in my own raven language – or so my tame sweetheart tells me. He was so lively

and confident; he hadn't come to woo the princess, he declared, only to hear her

wise conversation. He liked it very well, and she liked him."

"Oh, that was certainly Kay," said Gerda. "He was so clever, he could do mental

arithmetic, with fractions! Oh, do please take me to the palace."

"That's easily said," replied the raven, "but how is it to be done? I must talk to my tame sweetheart about it; she'll be able to advise us, I have no doubt, for – let me tell you – a girl like you would never be allowed to enter in the regular way."

"Oh, I shall get in," said Gerda. "When Kay knows I am here he'll come straight out and fetch me."

"Well," said the raven, waggling his head, "wait for me by the stile." And off he flew.

It was late in the evening when he returned.

Ra-a-ax! Ra-a-ax!" he cawed. "I'm to give you my sweetheart's greetings, and here's a piece of bread from the kitchen; there's plenty there, and you must be hungry. It's impossible for you to get into the palace as you are, without even shoes on your feet; but don't cry. My sweetheart knows a little back staircase that leads to the royal bedroom, and she knows where to find the key!"

So they went into the garden, and along the avenue where the leaves were falling, leaf after leaf; then, when all the lights in the palace had gone out, one by one, the raven led little Gerda to a small back door.

Oh, how Gerda's heart beat with hope and fear! It was just as if she were about to do something wrong – yet all she wanted was to find out if the boy really was little Kay. Oh yes, he must be Kay; she could see him in her mind so vividly with his bright clever eyes and smooth flowing hair; she remembered the way he used to smile when they sat together at home among the roses. Oh, he would surely be glad to see her, to hear what a long way she had come for his sake, and to know how grieved they had all been at home when he never returned. She trembled with fear, and hope.

They had now reached the staircase where the tame raven was waiting; a little lamp was glimmering on a stand. Gerda curtseyed, as her grandmother had taught her.

"My fiancé has spoken most charmingly of you, my dear young lady," said the tame raven, "and your life history, as we may call it, really touches the heart. If you will kindly take the lamp, I will lead the way. Straight on is best and shortest – we are not likely to meet anyone."

"Yet I can't help feeling that someone is following behind," said Gerda. And indeed, something did seem to rush along past her; it looked like a flight of shadows on the wall, horses with thin legs and flowing manes, huntsmen, lords and ladies on horseback.

"Those are only dreams," said the tame raven. "They come and take the gentry's thoughts on midnight rides and that's a good thing, for you will be able to observe them more safely while they are asleep. But I hope that you will show a thankful heart if you do rise to fame and fortune."

"Now, now, there's no need to talk about that," said the woodland raven.

They entered the first room, where the walls were hung with rose-coloured satin embroidered with flowers. Here, the dreams were racing past so swiftly that Gerda could not distinguish any one of the lords and ladies. Each hall that she passed through was more magnificent than the one before; then, at last, they arrived at the royal bedroom.

The ceiling was like the crown of a palm tree, with leaves of rarest crystal; and hanging from a thick gold stem in the centre of the floor were two beds, each in the shape of a lily. One was white, and in this lay the princess. The other was scarlet – and in this Gerda knew that she must look for little Kay. She turned one of the red leaves over and saw a boy's brown hair. It was Kay! She cried his name aloud, holding the lamp near his face; the dreams on their wild steeds came whirling back to the sleeper; he woke – he turned his head – it was not little Kay.

No, it was not little Kay, though the prince too was a handsome boy. And now the princess looked out from the white lily bed and asked what was happening. Little Gerda wept as she told her story, but she did not forget to speak of the ravens and their kind help.

"You poor child," said the prince and princess, and they praised the ravens, adding, though, that they must not do it again. This time, all things considered, they would be given a reward.

"Would you like to fly away free?" the princess asked. "Or would you like a permanent place as Court Ravens, with all the odds and ends you want from the kitchens?"

Both the ravens bowed, and prudently chose the permanent place, for they had to think of their old age. "It's a good thing to have something by for a rainy day," they said. The prince stepped out of his bed so that Gerda could sleep in it – and who could do more than that? As Gerda slept, the dreams came flying back – but this time they looked like angels; they seemed to be drawing a sledge, on which Kay was sitting, nodding at her. But this was only a dream, and it vanished as soon as she woke.

The next day she was dressed from top to toe in silk and velvet.

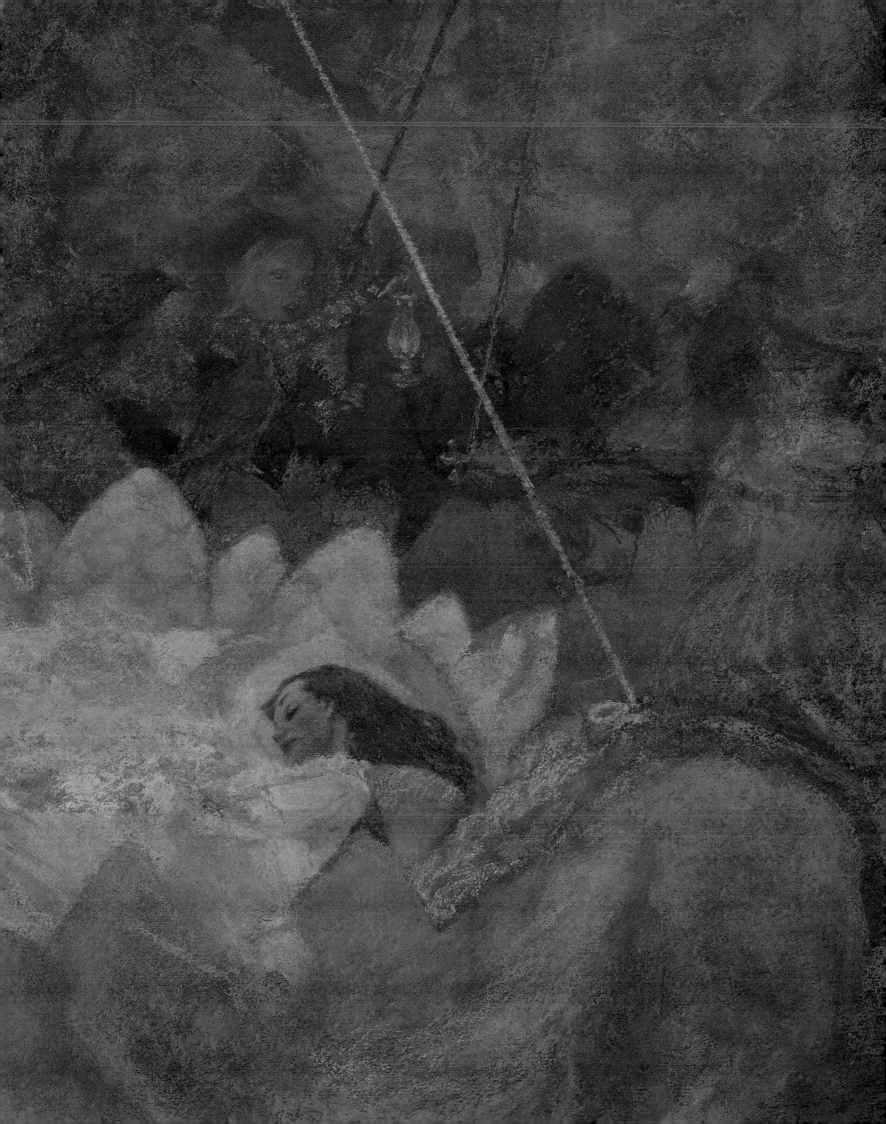

She was invited to stay at the palace and pass delightful days, but she begged to have just a little carriage with a horse to draw it, and a pair of boots small enough for her feet; with these she could drive out into the wide world and seek little Kay.

She was given not only boots, but also a muff. And when she was ready to leave, in beautiful fine warm clothes, a new carriage of pure gold drew up before the door; on it the coat of arms of the royal pair glistened like a star. Coachman, footmen and outriders – for there were outriders too – all wore gold crowns. The prince and princess personally helped her into the carriage and wished her good luck. The forest raven, who had now married his sweetheart, came along for the first twelve miles or so; he sat beside her, for he could not bear travelling backwards. The tame bird stood in the gateway flapping her wings; she didn't go with them because too much rich palace fare had given her a headache. The inside of the coach was lined with iced cake and sugar candy, while the space beneath the seat was packed with fruit and ginger nuts.

"Farewell! Farewell!" cried the prince and princess, and little Gerda wept. So did the raven, and in this way they passed the first few miles. Then the raven said his own goodbye, and that was the hardest parting of them all. He flew up into a tree and flapped his black wings as long as he could see the carriage, which gleamed as bright as the sun ❋

PART FIVE
The Little Robber Girl

———

THEY DROVE THROUGH THE DARK FOREST, but the carriage shone like a fiery torch; it dazzled the eyes of the robber band – they could not bear it.

"It's gold! It's gold!" they roared. Then, rushing forward, they seized the horses, killed the outriders, coachman and footmen, and dragged little Gerda out of the carriage.

"She's plump; she's a dainty dish; she's been fed on nut kernels!" said the old robber woman, who had a long bristly beard and shaggy eyebrows hanging over her eyes. "She's as tender and sweet as a little fat lamb. Yum, yum! She'll make a tasty dinner!" She drew out a bright, sharp knife, which glittered quite dreadfully.

"Ouch!" screeched the hag all at once. She had been bitten on the ear by her own little daughter who hung on her back, and who was so wild and mischievous that she was quite out of hand. "You loathsome brat!" said her mother, and forgot what she had meant to do with Gerda.

"She shall be my playmate," said the little robber girl. "She shall give me her muff and her pretty clothes and sleep with me in my bed." And so spoilt and willful was she that of course she had her own way. She got in the coach with Gerda, and away they drove, through bush and briar, deeper and deeper into the forest. The little girl was no taller than Gerda, but much sturdier, with broader shoulders and darker skin. Her eyes were quite black, with a curious look of melancholy in them. She put her arm around little Gerda and said, "They shan't kill you – not as long as I don't get cross with you. You're a princess, I suppose?"

"No," said Gerda, and again she told all her adventures, and how fond she was

of little Kay. The robber girl watched her seriously, and nodded her head. "They shan't kill you even if I do get cross with you," she said. "I'll do it myself." Then she dried Gerda's eyes and put both her hands into the pretty muff, which was so soft and warm.

Suddenly the carriage stopped; they had reached the courtyard of the robbers' castle. Its walls were cracked from top to bottom; crows and ravens were flying out of the gaps and holes, while huge hounds, each one looking as if he could swallow a man, leapt high into the air; but not a single bark came from them, for that was forbidden. In the great old hall, cobwebbed and black with soot, a large fire burned on the stone floor; the smoke drifted about under the roof, trying to find its own way out. A vast cauldron of soup was bubbling away; hares and rabbits were roasting on turning spits.

"Tonight you shall sleep with me and all my pets," said the robber girl. First they had something to eat and drink, then they went over to a corner where straw and blankets were scattered. Above them, in holes and on ledges, about a hundred pigeons were roosting; they seemed asleep but a slight stir ran through them when the little girls appeared.

"They're mine – all of them," said the little robber girl. She seized one of the nearest, took it by the legs, and shook it until it flapped its wings. "Kiss it!" she cried, waving it in Gerda's face. Then she pointed to some wooden bars nailed over a hole above their heads. "Those are woodland riff-raff, both of them. They'd fly off in a flash if they weren't locked up. And here's my special sweetheart, Bae." She pulled a reindeer forward by the horn; it was tethered to the wall, with a shiny copper ring round its neck.

"He's another one who'd fly off if we didn't keep him prisoner. Every night I tickle his neck with my sharp knife – he doesn't care for that!" And, drawing a long knife out of a crack in the wall, she ran it lightly across the reindeer's neck. The poor creature struggled and kicked, but the robber girl laughed, and pulled Gerda down with her under the rug.

"Are you taking that knife into bed with you?" Gerda asked, as she looked at it nervously.

"I always sleep with a knife at hand," said the little robber girl. "You never know what may happen. But now tell me again about little Kay and why you came out into the wide world." So Gerda told her tale once more, from the very beginning, and the woodpigeons moaned in the cage, and the other pigeons slept. Then the little robber girl fell asleep too, one arm around Gerda's neck, the other holding the knife; you could hear that she slept from her breathing. But Gerda couldn't even close her eyes, not knowing whether she was to live or die. The robbers sat round the fire and drank and sang, and the robber woman turned somersaults. It was a frightful sight to behold.

Then all at once the woodpigeons cried, "Rr-coo! Mm-coo! We have seen little Kay! A white hen was carrying his sledge, and he was sitting in the Snow Queen's carriage, which swept low over the forest where we lay in the nest. She breathed down on us young ones and all except the two of us here froze to death. Rr-coo! Mm-coo!"

"What are you saying up there?" cried Gerda. "Which way did the Snow Queen go? Can you tell me?"

"She must have been making for Lapland, for you'll always find snow and ice there. You ask the reindeer; he's sure to know."

"Yes, it's a land of ice and snow; everything there is lovely and pleasant," the reindeer said. "You can run and leap to your heart's delight in the great shining valleys. There the Snow Queen has her summer palace, but her real home is in a castle far, far off towards the North Pole, on an island called Spitzbergen."

"Oh, Kay, poor Kay!" sighed Gerda.

"Lie still, you," said the robber girl, "or you'll get my knife in your middle!"

When morning came, Gerda told her all that the woodpigeons had said. The little robber girl looked very grave, but she nodded and said, "Never mind – never mind; it's all one... Do you know where Lapland is?" she asked the reindeer.

"Who should know better than I?" said the reindeer, and his eyes shone at the thought of it. "I was born and bred in that land; once I could leap and play freely there in the snowfields."

"Listen to me," said the robber girl to Gerda. "All our menfolk are out. My old ma's still here and here she'll stay, but later in the morning she'll take a swig from that big bottle and after that she'll have forty winks. Then I'll see what I can do for you." She jumped out of bed, ran across to her mother, pulled her by the beard and called, "Good morning, my dear old nanny goat!" Her mother flicked her on the nose, making it quite red and blue – but it was all for sheer affection.

Then, when her mother had had a drink from the bottle and was taking a nap, the robber girl went over to the reindeer. "I'd love to go on teasing you a few more times with that sharp knife of mine because you always look so funny when I do – but never mind, I'm going to set you free so that you can run to Lapland. But you must put your best foot foremost and take this little girl for me to the Snow Queen's palace, where her playmate is. I expect you've heard her story; she was talking loudly enough, and you are always one for eavesdropping."

The reindeer leapt for joy. The robber girl lifted Gerda onto his back, taking care to tie her firmly on, with a little cushion for a seat.

"You'll be all right," she said. "Here are your fur boots – you'll need them in that cold – but I shall keep your muff; it's far too pretty to lose. Still, you won't have to freeze; here are my mother's big gloves. They reach right up to your elbows. Shove your hands in! Now they look just like my ugly old mother's!"

Gerda wept with happiness.

"I can't stand that snivelling," said the little robber girl. "You ought to be looking really pleased. Here are two loaves and a ham, so you won't starve." These provisions were tied to the reindeer's back. Then the little robber girl opened the door and called in all the big dogs; after that she cut the rope with her knife and said to the reindeer, "Off you go! But take good care of the little girl!"

Gerda stretched out her hands in the enormous gloves and called "Goodbye!" to the robber girl, and the reindeer sped away past bush and briar, through the great forest, over marsh and moor, and the wide plains, as swiftly as he could go. The wolves howled; the ravens screamed; the sky seemed

filled with sneezing, crackling noises – *schooo, schooo! piff, piff!* –

each time with a glow of red. "Those are my dear old Northern Lights," said the

reindeer. "Aren't they beautiful!" Faster and faster he ran, through the night, through

the day. The loaves were finished, and the ham – then they were in Lapland ✳

PART SIX

The Lapland Woman and the Finmark Woman

⚡

THEY STOPPED AT A LITTLE HUT, a wretched place; the roof nearly touched the ground and the door was so low that the family had to get down on all fours to crawl in and out. Nobody was at home except an old Lapp woman, who was frying fish over an oil lamp. The reindeer told her Gerda's story, but first it told its own, which seemed the more important. Gerda was too frozen with cold to speak at all.

"Oh, you poor things!" cried the Lapland woman. "You've a long way to go yet. You still have several hundred miles to cross before you get to Finmark – that's where the Snow Queen is just now, sending off those fireworks of hers every night. I'll write you a few words on a piece of dried codfish – I've got no paper – and you take it to the Finn woman living up there. She can tell you better than I can what to do." And so, when Gerda was properly warm and had had some supper, the Lapland woman wrote some words on a piece of dried cod and told Gerda to take good care of it. Then she fastened her on the reindeer's back again, and off they sped. *Schooo, schooo! Crack! crack!* came the noises from the sky, and all night long the glorious Northern Lights flashed violet blue. At last they arrived in Finmark and knocked on the Finn woman's chimney, for she hadn't even a door.

Inside it was so swelteringly hot that the Finnwoman wore hardly a stitch of clothing. She was small and dumpy, with a brownish skin. The first thing she did was to loosen little Gerda's clothes, and take off her boots and thick gloves; then she laid a piece of ice on the reindeer's head; then studied what was written on the dried-fish letter. She read it three times; after that she knew it by heart, and she dropped it into the cooking pot, for she never wasted anything.

The reindeer now told his story, and after that little Gerda's; and the Finn woman's wise eyes twinkled, but she didn't say a word.

"Ah, you're so clever," said the reindeer. "I know you can tie up all the winds in the world with a single thread; when the captain undoes the first knot he gets a fair wind; if he undoes the second, then gusts begin to blow; if he undoes the third and fourth, a gale roars up that hurls down the forest trees and wrecks the ship. Won't you make this little girl a magic drink that will give her the strength of twelve men, so that she can overcome the Snow Queen?"

"The strength of twelve men?" said the Finmark woman. "A lot of good that would be!" She went over to a shelf and took down a rolled-up parchment. She opened it out; strange letters were written on it, and she read so intently that the sweat ran from her brow like rain.

But the reindeer went on pleading so hard for little Gerda, and Gerda looked at her with such tearful, beseeching eyes, that once again she turned her gaze on them.

Then, drawing the reindeer into a corner, she put fresh ice on his head and whispered in his ear: "Little Kay is with the Snow Queen, sure enough; he finds everything there to his liking, and thinks that he's in the finest place in the world – but all that is because he has a splinter of glass in his heart, and another in his eye. These must come out or he'll stay bewitched, and the Snow Queen will keep her hold over him for ever!"

"But is there nothing that you can give little Gerda to break that hold?"

"I cannot give her greater power than she has already. Don't you see how great that is? How men and beasts all feel that they must serve her? How far she has come in the wide world on her own bare feet? She must not learn of her power; it comes from her own heart, from her being a dear and innocent child. If she can't find her own way into the Snow Queen's palace and free little Kay, there is nothing that we can do to help. Now! About ten miles further north is the edge of the Snow Queen's garden. You can carry the little girl as far as that, then put her down by the big bush with red berries, standing in the snow; don't stay gossiping, but hurry back here." With that, the Finn woman lifted little Gerda onto the reindeer's back, and off he dashed as fast as his legs could go.

"Oh! I've left my boots behind! And my gloves!" cried little Gerda. She felt stung by the piercing cold. But the reindeer dared not stop; on he ran till he came to the big bush with the red berries. There he put Gerda down, and kissed her on the lips; as he did so, great shining tears ran down the poor animal's face. Then he turned and sped back as fast as he was able.

And there was poor Gerda, without boots, without gloves, in the midst of that terrible icy land and its piercing cold.

She started to run forwards, but a whole regiment of snowflakes appeared in front of her. They had not fallen from above, for the sky was quite clear, sparkling with Northern Lights. These flakes came running along the ground, and the nearer they came the larger they grew. Gerda remembered how strange and wonderfully made the flakes had seemed when she'd looked at them through the magnifying glass. How long ago that was. But these were far bigger and much more frightening – they were the Snow Queen's frontier guards. They had the weirdest, most fantastic shapes. Some were like huge wild hedgehogs; others were like knotted bunches of snakes writhing their heads in all directions; others were like fat little bears with icicles for hair. All of them were glistening white; all were living snowflakes.

Then little Gerda began to say the Lord's Prayer, and the cold was so intense that she could see her own breath; it rose from her mouth like a cloud. The cloud became thicker and thicker, and took the form of little bright angels who grew in size the moment they touched the ground. On their heads were helmets; in their hands were spears and shields. By the time Gerda had finished her prayer, she was encircled by a whole legion of these spirits. They struck out at the dreadful snow-things, shattering them into hundreds of pieces, and Gerda was able to go on her way without fear or danger. The angels patted her feet and hands so that she hardly felt the biting cold, and she hurried on towards the Snow Queen's palace.

But now we must see how little Kay was faring. Whatever his thoughts, they were not of Gerda; he certainly did not dream that she was just outside the palace ❄

PART SEVEN
What Happened
at the Snow Queen's Palace
and What Took Place After That

———❖———

THE PALACE WALLS WERE OF DRIVEN SNOW, and the doors and windows of cutting wind. There were over a hundred halls, just as the drifting snow had formed them; the largest stretched for miles. All were lit by the brilliant Northern Lights. They were vast, empty, glittering, bleak as ice and deathly cold.

In the very midst of the palace there was a frozen lake; it had split into a thousand pieces, but each piece was exactly like the next, so that it seemed not an accident but a cunning work of art. The Snow Queen always sat in the centre of this lake whenever she was at home; she used to say that she was on the Mirror of Reason, the best – indeed, the only glass that mattered – in the world.

Little Kay was quite blue with cold; in fact, he was nearly black. But he never noticed, for the Snow Queen had kissed away his shivering and his heart was hardly more than a lump of ice. He was busily dragging about some sharp flat pieces of ice, arranging them in every possible pattern. What he was trying to do was to make a special word, and this he could never manage, try as he would. The word was ETERNITY. For the Snow Queen had said to him, "If you can spell out that for me, you shall be your own master, and I'll make you a present of the whole world, together with a new pair of skates." But he still could not manage it.

"Now I must fly off to the warm lands," said the Snow Queen.

"I want to take a peek into the black cauldrons." (She meant the volcanoes, Etna and Vesuvius.) "I shall whiten their tops a little; it does them good after all those lemons and grapes."

Off she flew, and Kay was left quite alone in the vast, empty hall, gazing at the pieces of ice and thinking, thinking, until his head seemed to crack. There he sat, stiff and still; anyone might have thought that he was frozen to death.

It was just then that little Gerda stepped into the palace through the great doors of cutting winds. But she said her evening prayer, and the cold winds dropped as if they were falling asleep. She entered the vast, cold, empty hall – and there was Kay! She knew him at once; she rushed towards him and flung her arms about his neck, crying, "Kay! Dear little Kay! I've found you at last!" But he sat there quite still, stiff, and cold.

Then Gerda began to weep hot tears; they fell on his breast and reached right through to his heart. There, they thawed the lump of ice and washed away the splinter of glass. Kay looked up at her, and she sang the verse they used to sing together.

"In the vale the rose grows wild;
Children play all day –
One of them is the Christ-child."

Then tears came into Kay's eyes too. And, as he cried, the second splinter of glass was washed away; now he could recognize her, and he cried out joyfully:

"Gerda! Dear little Gerda! Where have you been all this time? And what has been happening to me?" He looked around him.

"How cold it is! How huge and empty!" The air was so filled with their happiness that even the pieces of ice began dancing for sheer delight, and when they were tired and lay down again they formed the very word which the Snow Queen had told Kay to make – the one for which he would be his own master, and be given the whole world, and a new pair of skates.

Then Gerda kissed his cheeks, and their colour came back to them; she kissed his eyes, and they shone like hers; she kissed his hands and feet, and he was well and sound, and warm, the Kay she had always known. The Snow Queen could now come back as soon as she liked; Kay's sign of release was there, laid out in shining letters of ice.

Hand in hand, they walked out of the great, echoing palace. Wherever they went the winds were still and the sun broke out. When they reached the bush with the red berries, there stood the reindeer, waiting for them. With him was a young doe, and she gave warm milk to the boy and girl. Then the reindeer and the doe carried Kay and Gerda first to the Finmark woman, where they warmed themselves in the hot room and were given advice about the journey home, and then to the Lapland woman. She had made new clothes for them, and had prepared a sledge.

The reindeer and the doe bounded right up to the borders of the country. There, Kay and Gerda could see the first green shoots of spring coming out of the ground; the sledge could go no further, and the reindeer and the Lapland woman had to return to the north. "Farewell! Farewell! Goodbye! Goodbye!" said each and all.

The first little birds of spring began to twitter; the first green leaves appeared on the forest trees, and through the woods came a young girl riding a splendid horse. Gerda knew that horse, for it had been harnessed to her golden coach. The young girl had a scarlet cap on her head and pistols at her side. She was the robber girl!

She was tired of home life, she told them, and was making for the North; if she did not like it there, she would try some other direction. She recognized Gerda at once and Gerda recognized her; they were both delighted to meet each other again.

"You're a fine one to go straying off like that!" she said to Kay. "I wonder if you deserve to have anyone running to the ends of the earth for your sake!"

But Gerda patted her cheek and asked after the prince and princess.

"They've gone travelling to foreign parts," said the robber girl.

"And the raven?"

"Oh, the raven's dead," she replied. "His tame sweetheart's a widow now and

wears a piece of black wool on her leg. She's always moaning and groaning, but it doesn't mean a thing. Now you tell me your adventures, and how you managed to find him." And Gerda and Kay both told their separate tales.

"Well, well, well. Today's mishap is tomorrow's story," said the robber girl. She took each of them by the hand, and promised that if she ever passed through their town she would pay them a visit. Then she rode away, into the wide world.

But Kay and Gerda went on, hand in hand. As they went, the spring flowered round them, beautiful with blossoms and green leaves. They heard the church bells ringing; they saw ahead the towers and walls of a city; they were nearing home.

And they entered the town, and went up the stairs of the grandmother's house, and into the room near the roof, where everything stood just where it was before, and the clock still said "Tick tock", and the hands still marked the hours. But as they went through the door they noticed that they themselves had grown; they were not young children. The roses in the wooden boxes were flowering at the open window, and out there were their own little wooden stools. Kay and Gerda sat down on them and held each other's hands. The terrible, icy splendour of the Snow Queen's palace had slipped away from their minds like a distant dream. Grandmother sat beside them in the heavenly sunshine and read to them from the Bible. "Except ye become as little children, ye shall not enter into the Kingdom of Heaven."

Kay and Gerda looked into each other's eyes, and at once they remembered the old song, and saw its meaning:

"In the vale the rose grows wild;
Children play all the day –
One of them is the Christ-child."

So there they sat together, the same children still at heart. And it was summer, warm, delightful summer... ❊